LOVERS
AND
AGNOSTICS

BOOKS BY KELLY CHERRY

Sick and Full of Burning
Lovers and Agnostics
Relativity
Augusta Played
In the Wink of an Eye
The Lost Traveller's Dream
Natural Theology
My Life and Dr. Joyce Brothers
The Exiled Heart
God's Loud Hand

CHAPBOOKS

Conversion
Songs for a Soviet Composer
Benjamin John
Time Out of Mind

KELLY CHERRY

LOVERS
AND
AGNOSTICS

CARNEGIE MELLON UNIVERSITY PRESS
PITTSBURGH 1995

ACKNOWLEDGMENTS

"Benjamin John" was published in its entirety in *The Carolina Quarterly*; selections appeared in *Coraddi, The Greensboro Reader*, and *The Greensboro Review*.

"A Lyric Cycle" appeared in *The Greensboro Review*. The composer Imant Kalnin has set the cycle for soprano solo.

Other poems in this collection have been published in *Amanuensis, Anglican Theological Review, Contempora, Counter/Measures, The Greensboro Reader, The Hollins Critic, Mill Mountain Review, Poetry: Points of Departure, Southern Poetry Review, Twigs, Wasatch Front,* and *Western Humanities Review*.

I am also indebted to Kenneth Rexroth, whose translation of *The Greek Anthology* I quote in "Benjamin John."

First Carnegie Mellon University Press Edition, February 1995

10 9 8 7 6 5 4 3 2 1

CONTENTS

A LYRIC CYCLE

LOVERS AND AGNOSTICS

Translation: After Catullus 1

Now to whom am I going
to give this neat, new little book?
It was just this very minute prettily polished
with a dry pumice stone . . .

To you, dear Cornelius.
For you did use to find my trifling verses
of some value, even back then
when you alone among Italians grandly dared
to unfold all time in three volumes.
How learned they were! and full of labor.

So take this, friend, for yourself—
such as it is.
And on my behalf beseech the muse:

May it endure a little longer than its author.

AMONG THE MIGHTY DEAD

They always must be with us,
or we die.

—John Keats,
"Endymion"

THE BRIDE OF QUIETNESS

My husband, when he *was* my husband, possessed
Electrifying energy, humor,
The vital heat of violent force compressed . . .
Contraries in a controlling frame. Few more

Creative and compelling men could fire
The clay I scarcely dared to call my soul.
Shapeless, lacking properties of higher
Existence, it was perfect for the mold

He cast me in: classic receptacle,
A thing for use but full of elegance,
An ode to Greece, forever practical,
Tellingly patterned with the hunt and dance.

My lines were lies; and yet he seemed to see
Aesthetic validation in my form.
I asked him not to draw away from me.
He said he feared he might commit some harm—

Some accidental, inadvertent hurt—
And shatter in an instant all the love
He'd poured out in the effort to convert
My ordinary mind to a work of

Art. And how he shuddered if I assumed
A new position or a point of view!
As if I were a royal vase entombed
After the ancient style, and the issue

Of my movement could only be a change
In where he stood, relative to his wife.
I must perdure inanimate and strange
And still, if he would justify his life.

For I was the object of his most profound
Research, the crafty subject of his thesis,
And all I had to do to bring him down
Was let my heart break into all those pieces

It ached to break into in any case.
Upon his graduation, when the guests
Had gone, and night was settling on his face,
Raising my voice above his dreams I confessed

That beauty held no truth for me, nor truth
Beauty, but I was made as much of earth
As I had been, barbaric and uncouth,
Enjoined to rhythm, shiftings, blood and birth,

And void of principle. He said he'd father
No children. I could hardly help knowing
That he'd be wrong to trust me any farther.
By sunrise it was clear he would be going

Soon. Now from time to time I see him here
And there. The shoulders have gone slack, the eyes
Conduct a lesser current and I fear
That when they catch me spying, it's no surprise

To him. He always found poetic justice
Amusing, and he knows I wait my turn.
The artist dies; but what he wrought will last
Forever, when I cradle his cold ashes in this urn.

12

ADVICE TO A FRIEND WHO PAINTS

Consider shy Cezanne,
the lay of the land he loved,
its dumbstruck vanity, polite and brute.
The bather in his sketchy suit.
The skull upon the mute pull of cloth.
In your taxing and tearing, tugging at art,
consider shy Cezanne.
His blushing apples.
His love of man.

DEATH COMES TO THOSE WHO KNOW IT

Lines written during the reign of the Colonels

Homer! I said, speaking to the Old One,
things are different now, the trees have thickened,
sunlight is scarcer, Greece grows cool to poets.

Virgil weeps with Dante, Chaucer cries,
patient Milton averts his eyes.
In the distance blind tyranny lies

over the earth like a dark cloud riven with rain.
I think truth will not shine again.
I think this chill deceitful mist had lain

in wait till democracy was done,
and now the sadder among us begin to sicken,
silence shrouds Olympus, and death comes to those who know it.

A SONG FOR SIGMUND FREUD

Did you think you could hide from me?
But I won't *let* you.
Too long I've loved your mad anger, soft,
Wry, unrelenting rationality.

Once in Vienna, when the rain fell,
I saw you sing
And munch on your syllables as if they were mushrooms.
You were always full of fear for something

In the dark that teased your throat
Like a dog.
I could have cooled and warmed you any autumn.
Oh but you made yourself remote

In a last resort. Be brave, mein Liebchen, I won't bite.
Look at my sunny face. I'm bright! I'm fun.
So kiss me, Siggy! . . . Hold me tight.
And I'll waltz with you when the Nazis come.

IN MEMORY OF ELAINE SHAFFER

Elaine Shaffer, flutist, d. 1973. Was married to
Efrem Kurtz, conductor of the Kansas City
Symphony Orchestra. She studied with William
Kincaid and inherited his platinum flute.

My sister, Ann Cherry, also a flute soloist, was
Kincaid's last protégée.

I

They lie—all those who, so smartly, insist
That any correlation can exist
Between meaning and music. There is none.
Only a point at which the audience
For both stands and reveals itself as one.

I was robbed of poetry and sense.
Skewed by false spring, a bright recrudescence
Had rouged the cover of the *Time* that lay
On the kitchen table, and shielding my eyes
From glare, I closed them tight against the way

The world reclaimed its weather, its winter skies,
And left me with my spindly pieties
Uprooted, ugly, mean, spotted and bare,
Inadequate. No wreath of these would do
For her who once wore laurel in her hair,

And had the seasons, and their changes too,
At her fingertips, and nonetheless knew
That neither perfect pitch nor intonation
Could revise that calendar of discord
Keeping time, in invisible notation,

To the beat of the Bach on which she soared
Above inconstant earth, moving toward
A harmony of the heavenly spheres,
A union of celestial sound and light,
That now must add, to forty-seven years,

The last, by which the rest reduce to tears.
The afternoon has turned to ash and night
Wraps me in sackcloth. And so I set my *Time*
Aside. Asleep, I hide from unnamed fears,
But dream of music rich with sense and rhyme.

II

These are among the few who do survive
In the subconscious: *Sappho*, fathomless
Still, *Heloise* and *Helen*, antithesis
Each to each, *Elizabeth*, and the incisive
Curie, fanning her radioactive
Fire into ash of lead with relentless
Logic. In the science of sleep, the rest
Are fuel for dreams in which some come alive.

Now music enters myth and takes her place,
Eternal, central, and accompanied
By all the arts and learning of these dead
Women whom we symbolically embrace,
As another of our sex, forever freed,
Wakes from life to this lament of the unliberated.

III

Why not I instead of her?
Answer that! But there's no answer
To injustice nor any anger

Sufficient to the day of death—
The concert in the blood, beneath
The bland appearance of the breath

Designed to modulate deceit.
Becalmed, but drifting in my seat
From aisle to aisle, I too may meet

That ancient music, blown ashore,
The suspiration of a score
So strange only Shaffer could explore

Its most difficult passages.
When she played, she traversed ages
Just by standing still on stages

From Kansas City to Europe's
Capitals, and lifting to her lips
The platinum prize among Pan's pipes

While blue and silver spotlights played
Tricks upon the eyes, to persuade
Her listeners of aural shade.

But what bold audience follows
The frenzy of a flute that knows
Its embouchure is Apollo's?

And as we plunge deeper into
That wise and weakened heart, the true
Terror advances into view:

Too soon! Too soon! *Ms. Kurtz—she dead!*
Tear out this tongue, I should have said,
Let my life be hers instead—

But all around, the far country
Holds itself apart from me.
Elaine alone penetrated this mystery.

IV

The obvious solution is, to say
What she did, without words, with her dying

Breath. But the syntax of a sonata
Allows no possibility for lying,

Unlike poetry, which must, if the truth
Is to mean anything beyond the jar

In the wilderness, a wheelbarrow,
A redundant rendering of facts which are

Plain enough even in Little Gidding.
And still, music is more than the timeless

Present, and much more than mere emotion,
Is mathematics, movement and gladness

Of noise. How could I hope to embody
Pure intention, song in speech, or her soul?

V

My own soul, such as it is, has consumed
My time and interest. Reading my work
In private, I prepare to lay siege to
My own stage, such as it is: an unnamed
Local college, as tame and green a field
As any poet ever ran wild in.
No savage grace, no exploration of
The farthest reaches of the mortal heart,
No appreciation of art as rape

Grows up here: Hydrangea of the brain,
A common disease of showy magazines
And unambitious academia,
Is proudly cultivated, while fever
Weeds wave their subtle, bright and terrible blossoms
Out of sight in an unseen wind.
                    Elaine,
Elaine! I am light-years away from you,
Examining my syllables and stops
Under a new moon, and smiling at deans,
And hushing up the nerves that interrupt
This concentration of intelligence
Upon illusion, matter over mind.
I think an auditorium transports
Even the grave to ecstasy, bringing
Together polar opposites: The sleeping light,
All reawakening, the explosion
Of birth, daring, sense and music arise
From our leaden earth in a harmony
As magical as alchemical gold
Or philosophy.
          O Elaine, Elaine,
In that progression toward the plane of spirit
You and I, however unalike, move
Hand in hand, the poet and musician,
Behind the curtain's formal bow, and know
That when it closes for the final time
Our audience has always been the same
Demanding dream, the shadowy critic
Whose fearful standard fathers us, sisters
In sound, related through our haunting chorus:
The silence in the wings that waits for us,

The silence in the wings that waits for us.

BENJAMIN JOHN

*Faber est quisque
fortunae suae.*

—Sallust

THE LIGHTFOOT BOYS

He and his friends took the town;
Together, they painted it red.
Sneaking slugs into Stanley's jukebox,
Benjamin John said:

"In Ithaca I used to roller-skate
Sometimes at the corner rink,
When I was a kid," and they slouched,
Embarrassed, over their drinks,

At this mention of death.
Then three struck out for Giorgio's,
And two to Maggie's Meals,
And one, sulky, stuck in Stanley's booth:
Because things go hard with youth.

BENJAMIN JOHN AND THE GREEN QUEEN

He nurses his pint on Washington Square.
Plainly, the cops figure, this is a dare
To be lightly taken.

Like a goggle-eyed rube he has been shaken
Down, down. He was oh so sorely mistaken
In highhanded Eileen,

Who, friend Curt called to say, last night was seen
Twirling with Earl; her eyes outshone the green
She fizgiggly wore,

And she was matchless. A fifth of a pint more
To go: Benjamin John studies the stars
As if to find

Some semblance to the image, in his mind,
Keen, green, and warm. Now, conclude the cops: time
They closed in.

Benjamin John, drunk, shamed, and elated,
Cries to himself that God knows,
The trouble he's seen nobody knows.
A pox on the Great Bear for its rutilant, lambent, polar light.

O to have been Ben ben Bijn!

THE WIND FROM THE NORTH
LIKE A HOOT OWL HAWKING
HORSE SENSE PUTS HIM DOWN

AT THE GREENSBORO ZOO

At dusk, at last
Crawling crabwise across
The sky, the Milky Way
Readies to waylay
Coxcombs and ghosts,
Night owls,

And himself: caught
Cold, he shudders
At his twenty years' boasts,
At how he niggled, how
Like an ass
Stalled and brayed.

He jilts natural
Passions
For an insular singular nave:
Against this slate,
Sparked sky,
Leaves like priests'-palms wave:
Blessèd he'll crouch
Cublike,
A still small voice in the dark cave

Of his mind: rise in spring
To sideswipe like Oriental guerrilla
Brash things.

A P.O.W. ASIAN WARLORD, ARISTOCRAT, SLIPS THIS POEM TO PFC B. JOHN

1
Skirting this field
Rain from the West
Slapped those low hills
Hemmed in by mist

2
Shoots of wild grain
Spring up again

The sun will shake off
Outworn rag-ends
Of clouds: as a moth
Sheds its golden
Spent chrysalis

. . . AND BENJAMIN JOHN LOOKS TO HIMSELF

The draft board said,
"You are wanted
Alive or dead."

Juggernaut Board
Mother
My friends
My foxy foe:
Let me protest

That I couldn't care less.
Hell like Heaven
Lies to the West.

THE GETAWAY

East of the sun,
West of the moon,
South from Tennessee,
Benjamin John
Lies loafing; but the wide brass bed
Like a plumped-up anecdote
Seems to say,
"You are a dream-ridden fool
Who is no exception nor any rule."
Benjamin John,
Riding the fevers of 3 A.M. ,
Yanks the top sheet over.
To this lackluster, easy, leggy girl
Stretched out in shadow,
He would say,
"Wash the anchovies,/While I pour the wine"
In the words of a crazy Greek,
Cynical, lyrical.
She sleeps in her grand and blockish bed,
Benjamin John.
O this dull indolence . . .
O this lack of clarity; *fuzzy* pretense . . .
Lack of rhythm, drama, sense . . .
He will pack his toothbrush;
Solo, straddle and spur a llama to Chile or Peru . . .

Mad as a hatter, like a child
He buries his face in her tangled hair
And wishes this small, wild prayer:
I'm hiding, I'm hiding, and no one knows where.

HIS FIRST EXPLORATION OF THE SEA MADE AT MIDNIGHT

Sportively,
he holds his breath: The bubbles spring
lightly above his head, slicing
the water-sheet . . .
     The firmament
thus is rolled back; above him, cold
is the airy aerie Heaven sent
to taunt him in his discontent:
From Chesapeake Bay upward, he sees
stars, stars, stars.

Algae, fishes,
scaly organisms sway, swat
Benjamin John; he sees he's not
a *lonely* monster . . .
     But comfort comes
colder than Job's, like that: fished for,
and mocked by the far, fair, and lum-
inous lashes of the sleeping sun.
A rocking in his stomach wrenches
wry his soul.

O wretchedly
he shoots for Up: The sandbank saves
his life! or less. His elbows graze
the solid shore . . .
     But Paradise,
the carrot strung before the beast,
dangles still out of reach. He lies,
sick and hungry, on the beach, sighs:
Isn't he purged? Why does he dream
wantonly
of skin diving among the stars?

THE GRADUATE SCHOOL OF ARTS AND SCIENCES

Money! my honey,
bangs the world around.
Ghosts of Veblen,
ghosts of Marx,
stalk the sun across that yard.

THE SUN

On any day with a very blue sky,
the Blue Ridge swells
from his rented book
as a rose
from his rent skull.

FOR ALICE, WHOM HE MARRIES ONE YEAR LATER: THE PROPOSAL

Long distance.
"How are you?" "Fine.
How are you?" "Fine."
Restlessly, restlessly,
Pines scrape the sky.

Silence. Then together.
"Sorry, you go on." "No,
You go on." "Sorry."
Looking off, he gathers
Night in his eyes.

In the dark room
He moves alone
Restlessly, restlessly.
Asleep he becomes
A drowned bird washed
Ashore, bill, plume
Pared to the bone,
A skeleton.

SNOWFLAKES

Last night the Ides of March
swooped,
not softly, down and settled
on his head; above the mean clack-cackle of wind he heard
wings of birds white,
shrill and unshakable: chilled to the bone,
he stationed his Florsheims on the furnace grate

and snores past one,
Monday: beyond the windowed bay
stretch
scores of dead Trumpeters, mute, who feather-footed fell
Sunday.
He wakes: *Storm's died down,*

serves the damned storm right, and he notes:
his slipsole scorched. O now see him
blush like a green acolyte, and now
gingerly he undertakes, obsequiously,

shoveling of snow from off the front porch.

HE AND HIS WIFE ENTERTAIN CERTAIN OF THE FACULTY

They file in, vague or cheery, band
By habit at the makeshift bar
Where ill at ease his wife disbars
(He knows) each from her no man's land
And nods and chats and shoves caviar
At them, since only the best is good
Enough for those she "cannot stand."

He backs away from her trumped-up pride:
Here are Thomson, Tucker,
Moomaw, and Steve his usual friend;
And he as well was once a fan
Of the Fabulous Toad, Stealer of Motor Cars.

HE TEACHES IN A GIRLS' SCHOOL AND DELIGHTS IN HIS PUPILS

No sooner does spring invade
The campus than everywhere
In sleeveless dresses birds
With Beatle pins, long hair,

Long arms, bare legs invite
His interest: He rates
Three pointed passes per day;
How should he hesitate,

Figuring so in their dreams
(Shy, defiant, designed),
To take them, at face value,
Pitching the Keynes he assigned

Aside . . . Aside he turns,
Sticking with the old high way,
Mouthing the same old text:
He's got, christ, bills to pay,

And his wife is due next month;
And he has their themes to grade,
Work to do. Work he meant
To do, and plans mislaid . . .

Half-heartedly, he upbraids
Himself for wishing in vain;
These children, he knows, hang on him
So long as he's unattained,

And chugging after the train
Of his thought, he thinks he is wise,
Distant, faithful: Lord, he deserves
A gold star, a prize . . . prize . . .

The sun assaults his eyes . . .

Crossing campus, he squints:
The sun assaults his eyes . . .

Sun-coppered arms, minted
Days ago, surround him
In the wilderness—pretty girls

Too young, too young, but then,
Someone has to teach them.

TO HIS DAUGHTER

Five years old:
Her dark hair holds
The light of the moon.
She scales his knee:
"If I should grow up,
Would you marry me?"
I will: but hurry,
I'll be a yellow, mellow, waning melody soon.

HE SUMMERS IN EUROPE BUT IN SECRET
SEARCH OF THE GREEN QUEEN:
NORFOLK FAREWELL

His wife: "Write often, lose weight.
        Your daughter'll be eight
        weeks older. Write often.
        Waves suck the hull of the ship."

Mr. John: "Goodbye. Goodbye."

Mr. John: "The hull of the ship."

Mr. John: "Waves suck the slow warm white sure hull."

        His book he works on, time to time,
not un-neatly packed, his three by five note cards
        stacked,
he pushes off, off, off, off, off, charily heaving off
        from Norfolk's nestling June: there

***

        his old desire dizzy
        with the smell of dust and honey-
        suckle mingling day-
        dream and revenge
        drained his mind of memory
        stuffed it up with tissue
        stars lugged long
        ago from N.Y.C. . . . fool, a
        fool, he groans,
        fool indomitably!

***

Benjamin John: One tried and trying soul
the wide north wind wrapped up
—and shipped to sea—

***

In his head her silk voice like a lead gong clangs. "Often."

HIS WIFE'S BIRTHDAY

She sups with him and bravely smiles;
And smiling back, he is perplexed
By age, and by her tendered sex,
By her loose dry skin, her juvenile
Bangs; that her hair is dyed to a Greek
Shade, her eyes are shadowed. How vexed
He is at the unsuccess of her wiles

Which yearly mocks him; her female fears
Paraphrastic, harped on,
Score his nerves like a scratched record
Until in self-defense he is bored,
Bored to tears.

A THRENODY FOR THEORISTS

The leaves want raking; four o'clock settles
A reddish glaze on the front-yard pinecones.

Benjamin John, slumped in his chair, scanning
The headlines, works slowly on his whiskey sour,

And frowns at statesmen and their paramours
And sniggers at the rumors over Hanoi

Skeptically,
Unruffled,

As day by day the fallout climbs; and China,
Spinning her silk, screens off the first-born sun.

TO HIS NEPHEW ENROLLED IN A SCHOOL FOR EMOTIONALLY DISTURBED CHILDREN

Ratface in the lamplight rocks,
Rocks . . . rooted in his own shadow.
Balder than a mushroom, longfaced

And sloopshouldered, small, small,
Crafty . . . but blocked by the rising
Red sky: Ratface founders at sea,

See Ratface. This is Ratface. Run,
Ratface, run . . . The very devil
Damns your dreams of lost Atlantis,

And before long, my hair will go
This strange man thinks; and if he could,
He would link into ladders your rubber sheets,
Flee with you to France, and by your side, frame
And fight the Napoleonic Wars.

DAYLIGHT

lolls upon his desk.
Sticky in steaming curls,

washed out, the thick, thin girl
who shuffles to his side

unleashes, in her eyes,
in how she ducks, shunts, shies,

the hell she sics on him.
(Christ. Nightly clutched,

in wordless dreams, she is made
Athena, fierce Lady of Freshman Themes.)

He listens to her tears,
and the class bell buzzes.

He sees, looking beyond her cursed whining eyes,
sun grazing on the dying grass.

TO HIS WIFE

His wife is dead.
He is divorced
From what she said,
From what she read:
Trollope, Roth,
Ruth. Bless Ovid.
He feels no pity,
Neither remorse;
But why has he got
This ache in his head?

THE NIGHT AFTER CHRISTMAS

Clearing a space on the windshield,
He angles down this winding street
Toward Park, and curses the fool speed
Limit that hounds him in to heel.
He can hardly see in the middle ground
Those mangy azaleas, whipped by the sleet;
Or make out where the clouds have wheeled.

At the end of the road, does he wonder
Resentfully, bitching
That he knocks too late, the given-up guest,
Why air, rain, fire, fate and the snowbound earth
Should forever steal his thunder?

O to have been Ben ben Bijn!

THE WIND FROM THE NORTH
LIKE AN OLD GOAT GRAZING
A TRAIL BUCKS HIM ASIDE

DRUNK, HE SHEDS A TEAR FOR THE LANDSCAPE

Here lies no one,
only the drab
delta, lowering
and sullen and dumb,
by down-
pours, over-
flows,
beat and stopped;
and near the river's mouth,
lies rudderless, lies unmanned,
a drabber craft—not
moored, not
salvaged, only—
lonely—
beached.
Beached.

"Let the earth/Which has borne us all,
bear you."

HIS STONED YOUNGER COLLEAGUE IN ENGLISH SPEAKS

When I review myself, I wink.
Steve Link is a ballsy fink.

How sad I am on Sunday.
I tend to drink.

I tend to drink.
In Camp I coo
To my wife.

"You've got that, what we ain't got any,
You're my Little Orphan Annie."

I scan her dogeared eyes, Ben.
So then she strips.

                    Weekly.

Come Monday,
I needs wise rise
To torture the truth of Kafka's lies.

. . . AND BENJAMIN JOHN LOOKS TO HIMSELF

The figgly wars
that gobbled me
have passed away
from gluttony
and a weak heart.
I'm tart.

A VISION

Light spread on shade,
Riding the wide wind down,
The Greek green queen streams
Suddenly like a falling star.
She sighs like a tired avatar.

In her fire-eating face, signs
Of use: what waxy vein! sunken
Cheek: his darling bright chick

Who from peck-pecking at her mirror
Fell prey for her own shrunk shrine.
The white line of her neck droops,

And still, slyly, unseen,
He flicks her a kind kiss.
Besides, she owes him that
For what she made him miss.

But wasn't pain sweet?

But doesn't she tax his patience now they meet?

The lady ever wore her hair upswept
Coiled to spring
Like a green snake
Rattling among rocks.

What good does it do us to mourn
For our sons when the immortal
Gods are powerless to save
Their own children from death?
                    —Antipatros

OCTOBER

GENTLE and without warning
ELEGANT
—like a small girl sidney in velvet beret—
fitfully,
light rain at evening sprays
his storm window: his studio window.
His son-in-law, gray-haired, lantern-jawed,
thin, hands him his glass: grave, *GRAVE*
boy of fifty years;
chee. Did sons-in-law like this one *FERRET*
for—god knows, god knows what they hunt for
in a dead wife's father. He objects (bearing
the glass and his to his *ONE*-man's bar),
he has his own teaser: but what screwed son-
in-law could see, no man is a man
until he like bow-legged Sarasate can bandy
an *OLD* tune about/in double time.
(He shrugs) And (He shrugs) he has no words.
He was born knowing none
and has *SHUFFLED* into his last years
knowing none
and cares less. How then should he content
a shook son-in-law who never trembled
nor giggled
when Markos, as was right,

45

as was *FINE*,
rightly concluded:

"So pour the whiskey and kiss my wife or yours."

Or did both women, hand-in-hand
Sometime ago, fanning out their long dark hair,
Rise wheeling through the night air,
And turn south, and disappear . . .

      Breaking out his better Scotch,
He scans himself in the mirror,
Mirror, on the wall;
He is not, now, surprised
By love or death or by the startling, silky
Rain or the Fall,

      And anyway (cheering
His own face and its workable disguise),
His turn, his turn will come; and dead,
Even this fool will have time to grow wise.
He draws the brown study drapes

      Against the rain . . .
He draws the brown drapes

        . . . rain, what remarkable . . . (sighs)
What rain . . .
What rain . . .

"What, Tom? I guess I was thinking
About something.

                    Yes.
Yes. No, no; nothing.

                It wasn't anything."

THE ROSE-LIPT GIRLS

Each day the past seems longer ago:
Facts, faces, figures fade
And perhaps he is not unafraid
At night, that they were never so:
Or where could all those flowers go?
. . . The wind in the willows, brushing
The moon, spanking the wild roses,
Foreshadows their full eclipse.

But for every Beauty he's forgotten,
There were two he kissed.

A BY-LINE: ON HIS CANCER

Wife and mother, father, daughter,
Each in death dispraises me.

At sunup, I start on scrambled eggs
And Old Crow: the bright sun brazes me
Into the model of an old man
At breakfast: but nothing dismays me,
Not truth nor art. Only that I own
Time still, and solitude, amazes me.

The trellis roses, damp, bud. I see
The milkman making rounds. Dear stern friends,
—It's nothing new, being without them—
In my turn, I've grown a secret fondness for
—Later on I'll prune the sycamore—
This oddest of my maladies that stays with me.

A LYRIC CYCLE

What of soul was left, I wonder,
when the kissing had to stop?

—Robert Browning,
    "A Toccata of Galuppi's"

SAPPHO

"When you left, I cried
fiercely. Then I died.

"Will you suffer my sorrow:
let me forgive you.
I will when the owl lights on the oak
sweep with my brush your loose hair
back.

"And love you in bed.
And wrap this sweet sheet
round you, until you
are dead."

SEPTEMBER

The wet west wind wrapped
us up;
red leaves rained

down your back.
Oh, you—
I

know who you are,
dragon
dragging your muffled fires
through the chilled woods.

IF YOU WERE AN ANGEL

If you were an angel,
I would laugh you out of heaven,
And set your hair on fire,
And your black eyes burning
Would bloom like a black flower.

ROSES

As I was a child,
You pampered me with roses.
In this airless room,
I shuffle their petals, and inhale
Their thick, dull, deadly, pink perfume.

COLD AIR

The colors of wind are cold.
    On a cold night, I read
Some books, and some books
    Are cold, but I read,

And in my head, I know I hear
    Gray grating words
Winged on an arctic wind.
    Absurd . . .

A SONG

How he loved me! trembled,
    if I touched his hand.
    I saw his quick eyes glittering
    in the night.
    I saw him strip off his skin.
And white bones clattering,
    he fled into the night.

BLUE AIR

Against the blue air,
    He floats muter than a ghost.
I watch his wavering there,
    Upon the air,

And wait for his words to fall
    On me, words I want most.
But he says nothing at all,
    But floats above the air.

IN THIS PINK DAWN

In this pink dawn,
My heart flares up and dies down.
Bright wind crackles around my ankles.
I held my tongue
When you went away.

MIDNIGHT

If I said I loved you,
It was because I was bored.
Or in an aimless moment,
I may have caught the mood of the moon
Making overtures toward a mockingbird.

END OF SUMMER

I could have sworn
I saw the leaves
changing color,

the west wind torn
from the sky and bunched
into a cloud.

I could have sworn
you scorched my sleep
like lightning.

CIRCE

"But as the fading sun clips you from my sight,
I will remember you.

"When you have gone,
the sun
like a silent song
will burn up the far side of night."

LOVERS AND AGNOSTICS

My love is of a birth as rare
As 'tis for object strange and high:
It was begotten by Despair
Upon Impossibility.

—Andrew Marvell,
"The Definition of Love"

ON WATCHING A YOUNG MAN
PLAY TENNIS

The male poets run, lifting their feet like pros.
Others fish, and then there are those
Whose driving force
Sends them to the sandtraps of an eighteen-hole course

In search of metaphor. I have no yen
For sun and sky and earth, no kin-
Ship for the sea.
The element of mind is quite enough for me,

And dreaming in the damp of poolside shade,
I let imagination wade
Through the shallow
Stretch of time beyond a bend of tanning elbow,

And burning thigh, to where the poet plays
A love game with my yesterdays.
I have no zest
For exercise, no yearning after limberness

For the sake of limb alone, but enjoy,
Girlishly, this energy of Boy
That seeks to know
The meaning of *mens sana in corpore sano.*

Turning on my side, I see the shadow
Of his racket on the court grow
Long and widen
Till its very silence trespasses on the Haydn

Which carries from the house, and I put down
My drink and move inside where sound
And light and drift
Of dinner's smells serve, albeit fleetingly, to lift

My spirits to a plane of praise upon
Which I can stand and frankly own
That I am tired,
And lazy, and will leave to others more inspired

The satisfaction of the outdoor sports.
A young man in his tennis shorts
Suffices to
Realign the balance of my brain and back so

That I am paralyzed with memory
Of verse and versifier. (Yet I
Remember when
I volleyed more than words with the artfullest of men.)

POEM TO A GIRLFRIEND

How can you judge!
You don't even know what it's like,
Don't know what it's like to have elbows made of water,
Hands that tremble, fat wet cheeks.
But I know.
I am a white moth beating against his beautiful, bright
Brain. I am pulp.
When the lights go out and the room fills up
With those leggy, grasping crawlers,
It's me they're after.

ELEGY FOR A DYED REDHEAD

A man, a Mason, speaks

Sitting, she
toys with this thing.
How her hair flickers and burns! . . . matches
the blush her cheek commands.

She is Chicago raging. She blows
hot, blows
cold. In the middle of the night,
we both are burning bright.

In the middle of the night I dreamed
she crumbled, ashes
raining on my head
like a storm of dust or curses.
I laid her down among the dead.

TRANSLATION: AFTER CATULLUS 8

So long, chicken.
Cuckold Catullus can crow now:
Now it is your turn to brood.
May the sky fall in on you!
You'll weep buckets: "Why not?
What is left for me?"
And who *will* kiss you now?
For whom will you spread your wings?
Whose roost will you perch on?
Whose will you be said to be,
When night falls, and quick tongues cluck,
Recounting blow by blow your barnyard tales?

Their cruel words stick in my craw.
But Catullus, this Catullus, holds his peace.
And he smooths his plumage
That once shone bright as the red sun.

TO CATULLUS—HIGHET

(A RESPONSE TO THE HIGHET TRANSLATION OF CATULLUS 70)

My lover says he'd want to lie with none
but me, even if Venus herself welcomed his wooing.
Oh yes! but what a man will say to an older woman,
    write it on thin air, read on the run.

TRANSLATION: AFTER CATULLUS 85

I both hate and love. And you think I can provide
   The reason I suffer myself to be torn two ways!
I only know that in my bones I feel *I* raise
   This cross on which I'm crucified!

A POET'S ADVICE

At night I count sheep;
   Years in the day.
(The former for sleep.)
   Hold madness at bay

By stepping on cracks.
   Always I keep
Cerberean dogs
   To tend my sheep.

THE UNIVERSE CREATING ITSELF

Night.
I hunger after light,
The taste of radiance and ray—
I eat energy by the ion,
Swallow illumination,
Eschew quanta, drink pure
Wave. Only Nothing is sure.
Fulfillment is iffy; first I pray
For this chance to break my fast.
When I'm full I'm mass.

CARNEGIE MELLON
CLASSIC CONTEMPORARIES

Peter Balakian
Sad Days of Light

Marvin Bell
The Escape into You
Stars Which See, Stars Which Do Not See

Kelly Cherry
Lovers and Agnostics

Stephen Dobyns
Black Dog, Red Dog

Rita Dove
Museum
The Yellow House on the Corner

Stephen Dunn
Full of Lust and Good Usage
Not Dancing

Charles Fort
The Town Clock Burning

Tess Gallagher
Instructions to the Double

Brendan Galvin
Early Returns

Colette Inez
The Woman Who Loved Worms

Denis Johnson
The Incognito Lounge

X. J. Kennedy
Nude Descending a Staircase

Greg Kuzma
Good News

Larry Levis
The Dollmaker's Ghost

Thomas Lux
Sunday
Half Promised Land

Jack Matthews
An Almanac for Twilight

Dave Smith
The Fisherman's Whore

Maura Stanton
Snow on Snow
Cries of Swimmers

Gerald Stern
Lucky Life
Two Long Poems

James Tate
Absences

Jean Valentine
Pilgrims